NAZZY PAKPOUR

OWEN DAVEY

PLEASE DON'T BITE ME

FLYING EYE BOOKS

CONTENTS

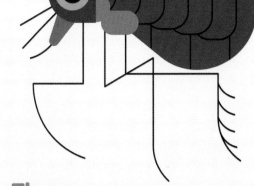

INTRODUCTION

Let's start with the basics, what exactly is an insect? An insect is an animal that has six legs, two eyes, two antenna, and three body parts.

A special group of scientists called entomologists have been studying insects for hundreds of years and they have learned all kinds of amazing things. Such as how while some insects like to feed on pollen (like butterflies), or plants (like grasshoppers) other insects have slightly more unusual tastes, and that's where you come in. Our bodies offer a delicious and unique menu of food for a vast variety of insects. These insects drink our blood, live in our homes, and even in our hair! They impact every aspect of our lives, from the clothes we wear, the pets we keep, to the homes we live in, and the way we store our food. Like tiny aliens living among us, each insect has its own unique body, home, and lifestyle. You have probably heard or seen most of these insects, but how much about them do you really know?

MOSQUITOES

You are sitting outside with your family enjoying a barbecue and watching a particularly beautiful sunset. But down by your ankles, under the table, something else is enjoying the sunset too ... All of a sudden the urge to scratch a certain spot becomes overwhelming. You scratch, and scratch again, and when the itch still won't go away you look more closely and notice that telltale raised red spot—a mosquito bite.

What are mosquitoes?

Mosquitoes are flying insects that live on land and in the water. With more than 3,000 different types of mosquitoes in the world, almost every animal on the planet suffers from mosquito bites, including us. These pesky insects are found everywhere on Earth except for Antarctica and Iceland, where the climate is just too harsh for them to survive!

Mosquitoes are never far from water because without it they can't complete their life cycle. Large numbers are often found around swamps and wetland habitats.

BLOODTHIRSTY FEMALES

Mosquitoes love blood! Our blood, and the blood of other animals, is rich in protein. If mosquitoes don't have protein they can't make eggs, which is why only female mosquitoes feed on blood! That is right, male mosquitoes are never going to bother you because they don't need to make eggs. So, if you have an itchy red bump on you, female mosquitoes are to blame.

Male mosquitoes feed on plant nectar found in flowers, the same stuff that bees and butterflies eat. Female mosquitoes will feed on nectar too, but only if they can't find any blood.

Male or female?

Say you notice a mosquito in your room . . . how can you tell if you have a bloodthirsty female mosquito or a gentle nectar-feeding male mosquito? What you need to do is get close enough to see their antennae. Male mosquitoes always have big fluffy antennae, while female mosquitoes have thin long antennae. This is because antennae are not only how mosquitoes smell, they are also how they listen! Antennae are the nose and ears of mosquitoes and male mosquitoes find their special lady friends by listening for the sound of their wings.

Female

Male

That whining sound you may have heard as a mosquito buzzes by your ear is the sound of a mosquito's wings flapping. Each species sounds slightly different because they flap their wings at different speeds during periods of flight—we call this wing beat frequency.

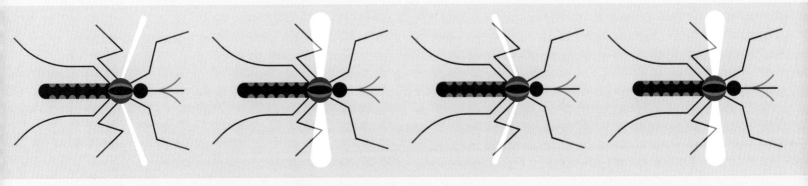

Many female mosquitoes will excrete out the water part of blood WHILE they are still feeding on you to maximize the amount of protein they can stuff themselves with. That means mosquitoes spit, feed, and pee on you at the same time and you never notice any of it . . .

11

STEALTH MODE

We've all had a mosquito bite, but have you ever wondered how it managed to sneak up on you, bite you, suck your blood, and fly off all before you even noticed it was there? Well, it turns out that mosquitoes have evolved sneaky mechanisms to find and bite their prey without being detected . . .

How do mosquitoes find you?

The short answer is you smell! I don't mean in the "I haven't showered for a week AND rolled around in mud AND rubbed rotten fish on myself" kind of smell. No, what I mean is the normal natural smell that all humans have and are putting into the world all the time. What a mosquito is smelling is not your stinky armpits but your breath, specifically the carbon dioxide (CO_2) in your breath. Even weirder, mosquitoes don't have noses. They smell with their antennae!

Antenna

A mosquito can smell CO_2 from 160 ft. away! That means a mosquito on the ground could smell you standing on the 5th floor balcony of a building.

Proboscis

How do mosquitoes bite you?

Mosquitoes are not actually biting you, what they are doing is poking you, with a teeny tiny straw mouthpart called a proboscis. That "straw" has evolved into the perfect shape for sucking your blood; it looks just like the beveled edge of a needle. But unlike a needle, you never feel the poke of a mosquito's proboscis. That is because before the mosquito starts feeding on you, it first spits into you. Tha's right, you heard me correctly, mosquitoes spit IN you!

Skin

Veins

And how do they bite you without you noticing?

Mosquito spit is magical and contains some pretty amazing stuff like chemicals that numb you, stop your blood from clumping to form a scab, and stop you from itching. All this so that you never notice a mosquito while it is feeding on you. Pretty sneaky, huh? Mosquitoes are nature's perfectly designed blood thieves; they can take a nice long sip of your blood, fill up their bellies, and fly away before you know what happened.

Full belly of blood!

Mosquitoes with full bellies can't fly well as they are too heavy for their little wings. They can barely lift off the skin after feeding and often have to go hide somewhere nearby. There, they wait until their food digests and passes through them before they take off again.

HOME SWEET HOME

This talented female mosquito has a nose for CO_2 and a taste for blood. She has taken a nice big ol' bellyful of blood from you without you noticing, but where does she go next?

First, her body breaks down the blood into proteins. These are reassembled to make mosquito eggs. She will then go looking for a calm bit of water to lay her eggs. Just like she can smell CO_2 with her antennae, she also has the ability to smell water (H_2O).

Adult female mosquitoes live for six weeks on average and can lay eggs every 3 to 4 days, which means that during her lifetime a single female mosquito can lay more than 1,000 eggs.

Mosquitoes lay their eggs in almost anything that holds water. Once she finds a suitable spot, she will land on the surface and lay around 100 eggs. So they don't sink and drown, the eggs stick together and float like a tiny raft.

MOSQUITO METAMORPHOSIS

Mosquitoes start out life as tiny wormlike creatures called larvae. These larvae are no bigger than the letter "i" in this book and they look and act nothing like an adult mosquito . . . not yet anyway. To become a fully formed mosquito they need to undergo a process called complete metamorphosis.

Bum breathers

A mosquito larva has a siphon. This is a part of its body that helps it to breathe underwater. It sticks out of the water, similar to a snorkel. But instead of breathing out their mouths, mosquito larva breathe out their bums. This is why the larva always have to stay close to the surface of the water.

← Siphon

Microscopic meals

Larvae dive down to feed on tiny living things in the water, like bacteria, yeast, and algae. They use their specialized brushlike mouth parts as nets to catch their food and sweep all that microscopic deliciousness into their mouths.

Armored bodies

Mosquito larva, just like all insects, have a hard outer shell called an exoskeleton. There is only so much space inside an exoskeleton, so when an insect runs out of space, they grow a bigger one and shed the smaller one. This process is called molting.

Larva grows so big, its exoskeleton cracks open.

Larva wiggles out of its old exoskeleton and inflates its new larger exoskeleton.

Larva waits for its exoskeleton to harden and off it goes.

Complete metamorphosis

A pupa is a stage in an insect's life cycle between larva and full-grown adult. When insect larva get big and fat enough they develop into a pupa. Inside the pupa incredible things are happening! The mosquito is melting down itself and completely remaking itself by growing eyes, antennae, wings, and a whole new fabulous adult mosquito body. When the new body is done, the pupa exoskeleton cracks open and an adult mosquito emerges. This type of change finishes the complete metamorphosis.

Mosquito pupae breathe through snorkels on their back called trumpets.

You might be more familiar with the complete metamorphosis a caterpillar goes through to become a butterfly but lots of other kinds of insects undergo this process, including bees, beetles, cockroaches, and flies.

Even penguins, otters, and pigs have lice! In fact, the only animals that don't have lice are platypuses, echidnas, pangolins, and cetaceans. Lice have been around for so long, you can even find a fossil record of them!

LICE

Have you ever had an itch you just can't get rid of? Where you scratch your head and immediately have to scratch your head again. All the way to school, you scratch, and scratch and scratch. But you don't just feel itchy, you also feel like something is moving on your head! Maybe you are scratching your head when you feel a crunch and realize you just squished an insect . . . on your head! What is going on? Well, it turns out you have lice!

What are lice?

Lice are tiny insects that are smaller than the tip of a pencil and live in the hair and feathers of animals. Since we are animals, we have lice that live in our hair too. Although it isn't pleasant to have lice, you are actually in pretty good company—nearly every bird and mammal on the planet has lice.

Lice (Lepidophthirus macrorhini) can survive on elephant seals that dive 6,500 ft. under water.

ONE OF A KIND

There are over 5,000 different kinds of lice, and lice, it turns out, are very picky about where they live. Why is that? Well, each one is specific to the fur of the particular animal it feeds on. So human lice would never live on a dog, and bird lice will never live on a human.

Snouts for sucking

To a louse your head is a tasty treat to feed upon, and what they feed upon is your blood! Lice use a sucking snoutlike mouth called a *haustellum* to drink your blood. The inner surface of their snout has tiny teeth for gripping your skin and helping the louse to hold on while it feeds. The outer part of the snout has tiny needlelike projections that are thrust into your skin and allow the louse to spit directly into you.

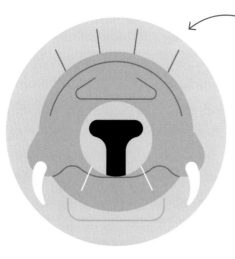

Haustellum

Special spit

Louse saliva numbs you so you don't feel them feeding, and stops your blood from clotting. Lice spit also makes you itch. It turns out most people are actually allergic to lice saliva so you feel itchy because of your body's reaction to the spit. It takes over 30 days for your body to develop an allergic response, which means some people can last a whole month unaware that lice are living in their hair!

Grab and don't let go

Lice have sharp claws at the end of their feet. These claws are specialized to hold on to a particular type of hair, fur, or feather. Human lice, have specially designed claws for holding on to our hair and they do not come off easily. You can shower five times a day, brush your hair for hours, go swimming, and shower five more times and these little insects would still manage to hold on!

Claws

Snout

Creepy crawlers

Lice don't have wings, so they can't fly and they can't jump either, so they can't hop onto you. But what they can do is crawl! Lice can move 9 inches in about one minute, which is pretty fast for something that is only 0.10 in. long. That is about the equivalent of a person who is 5 ft. tall moving 450 ft. in one minute.

Stork lice

Cockatoo lice

THE LIFE OF A LOUSE

While some insects live in different environments at different stages of their lives, lice spend their whole life in one environment. That means at some point you could have every stage of a louse's life cycle living in your hair!

Not-so-magical nymphs

The babies that hatch out of lice eggs are called *nymphs*. What is a nymph, you ask? It sounds like a magical fairy creature that lives in the woods, but sadly it is not. A nymph is the young stage of an insect that undergoes incomplete metamorphosis.

In incomplete metamorphosis, an insect egg hatches a small nymph. The nymph is a miniature version of the adult insect that will slowly grow bigger. As the nymph grows, it molts, or sheds its old exoskeleton when it becomes too tight. A louse nymph will go through three molts, before reaching adulthood.

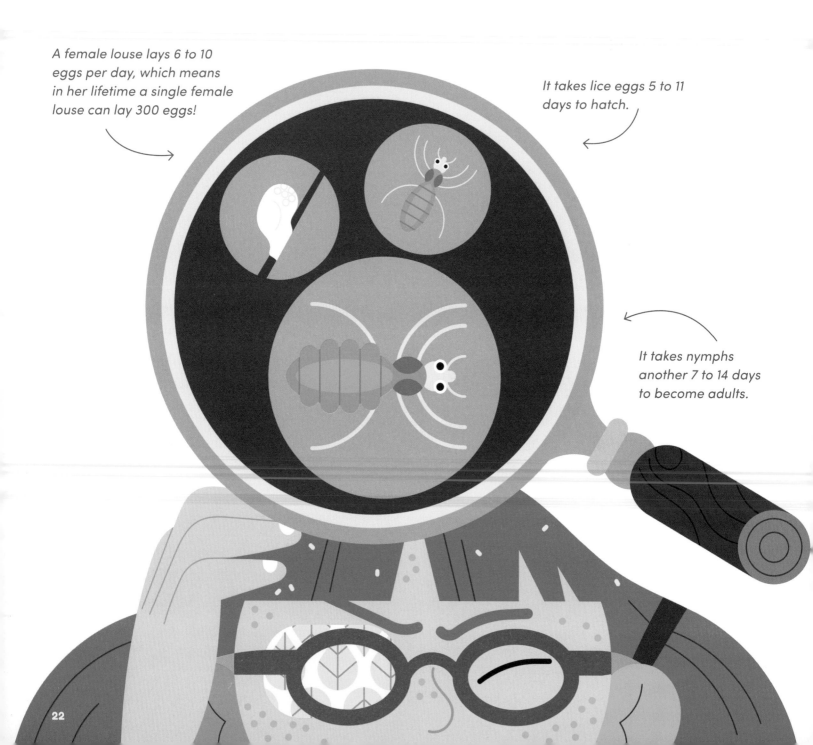

A female louse lays 6 to 10 eggs per day, which means in her lifetime a single female louse can lay 300 eggs!

It takes lice eggs 5 to 11 days to hatch.

It takes nymphs another 7 to 14 days to become adults.

Indestructible eggs

Those precious tiny eggs are glued on to individual strands of our hair about 0.4 in. from our scalp. They are so firmly attached that it is almost impossible to get them off. The glue is so similar to our hair that anything we might use to dissolve it would also dissolve our hair too. While the lice are inside their eggs, they are impossible to kill.

Insects that undergo incomplete metamorphosis all tend to live and feed on the same stuff which is why lice nymphs live in human hair just like their adult parents.

Psst—Don't worry! Having lice doesn't mean you are dirty, or bad, or did anything wrong. You just had a little bad luck and literally got stuck with these guys. It can happen to anyone, and probably has happened to almost everyone, including me!

THE LONG HISTORY OF LICE

Throughout much of human history, everyone, and I mean everyone, had lice. Think of your favorite historical figure and I can almost guarantee that they had lice. All it takes is a bit of bad luck, getting close enough to someone with lice to get a few to move from their head to yours, and now you've got lice. Luckily though, you can get rid of lice and surprisingly the tools and methods we use today haven't changed much from methods used thousands of years ago.

The word nitpicky, which means pointing out very minor mistakes in something, actually comes from the word nitpicking, which is the very tedious process of getting nits (lice eggs) out of someone's hair.

Inside ancient Egyptian tombs, archaeologists have found the remains of lice. They've also discovered ancient tomb paintings showing Egyptians picking lice from a child's hair. Ancient Egyptians tried to get rid of lice using various hair tonics or by picking them out.

The Chinese discovered that dried chrysanthemum flowers ground into a powder could be used to kill lice.

The word lousy actually comes from the word louse. The original meaning of it was "infested with lice." Over time it came to mean all the things a lice infestation can make you feel—ill or bad or disgusting.

Lice die very quickly (within 24 hours) if they are away from their food source and that food source is you! So, it is incredibly rare to get infected from things like hairbrushes, hats, pillows, or couches.

In Europe, nobles were taught the proper etiquette for disposing of one's lice and it was considered rude to scratch lice in public.

Today we get rid of lice by combing them out with a VERY fine-tooth comb. Even though the process is thousands of years old, nitpicking is still the best way to get rid of lice. In addition to lice combs we also use special lice killing medicines and shampoos.

Wasps range from big to teeny tiny with the largest being 2 in. long and the smallest only 0.0006 in. long.

WASPS

Who hasn't had the experience of sitting down at a picnic table on a beautiful sunny day to enjoy some food with friends only to have their food attacked by wasps.

What are wasps?

These insects are the less-friendly insect relatives of ants and bees. You can identify a wasp by the narrow waist of their third body part, the abdomen. Like a lot of animals, wasps use their bright yellow color as a warning to everyone . . . watch out I have a stinger! There are more than 100,000 different types of wasps and they live everywhere on the planet except Antarctica. Most of them live alone, don't sting, and have nothing to do with humans. Only a few specific types are considered pests to humans and even then, its only when they happen to build their nests near us.

WHAT DOES A WASP WANT TO EAT?

Most wasps (and humans) are omnivores, which means they eat a mixture of foods that come from plants and animals.

Adult wasps tend to eat things like flower nectar, fruits, or tree sap. Wasp babies (larvae) tend to eat other insects, meat, and fish. So, when a wasp is circling your hamburger, she is trying to bring food to the baby wasps back at the nest. Wasps primarily hunt other insects as food for their babies, so they are actually a great way to control the pests in your yards and spiders around the house.

Did you know worker wasps make baby food by pre-chewing the meat they collect before feeding it to their babies?

INSECT ARCHITECTS

Social wasps build amazing nests to live in with their families. In the wild, different types of wasps use parts of plants, mud, and secretions from their bodies to build their nests.

Paper nest

Mud nest

The type of wasp that people usually encounter make paper nests. These nests are made from wood fibers gathered from dead trees that wasps soften by chewing and mixing with their saliva (spit). This produces a wood pulp that the wasps then use to build their papery brown or gray nests. These nests are usually found attached to homes or trees near homes.

Wasp nests can be huge,
the largest ever recorded was
11.5 ft. tall and 18 ft. wide!

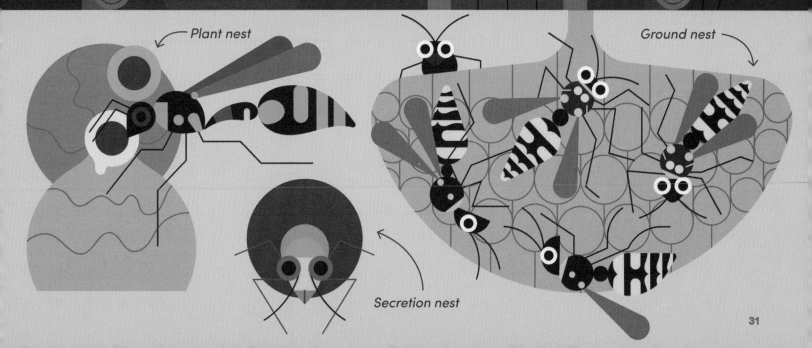

Plant nest

Ground nest

Secretion nest

A NEST FULL OF SISTERS

The wasps that most of us are familiar with are social insects. I don't mean social as in they love to throw parties and hang out with their friends. When scientists say an insect is social, it means they live in a group made up of their relatives.

Social wasps, sometimes called yellow jackets or hornets, live in a giant group made up of a single queen wasp that lays eggs, a few male wasps whose only job is to help make more babies, and lots and lots of sister wasps that do all the rest of the work. Can you imagine what your home would be like if you lived with 100 sisters? In a wasp community every sister has an assigned chore. The queen wasp lays eggs, some of the sister wasps stay in the nest to feed the babies, while other wasps are in charge of gathering food. In fact, a wasp community is very similar to a beehive, but minus the honey of course.

If you look inside a wasp's nest you will find a honeycomb hexagon pattern of little spaces, like tiny cribs, into which a wasp egg is laid.

Nest nursery

Wasps undergo complete metamorphosis, which means inside their cocoon they are melting down their worm body and building a whole new body complete with wings, antennae, and of course, their stinger! In the fall all the wasps in the nest will die except for a few queens. These queens will emerge in the spring to start the cycle again by building new nests and laying eggs.

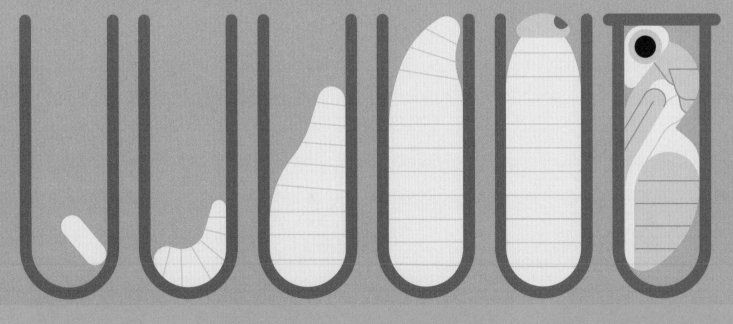

Baby wasps hatch out of eggs inside a wasp nest.

A few days later a small wormlike wasp larva will hatch.

Larvae are taken care of and fed by worker wasps for almost three weeks.

Once big enough, they will spin a cocoon inside their tiny hexagon crib within the nest!

WARNING SIGNS

Unlike mosquitoes, fleas, and lice, who all go to great effort to make sure you don't know they are biting you, wasps want you to notice them. That is why they are brightly colored, and it is why they have such a painful sting. It is their defense against things (like humans) that might want to kill them, and it is also how they hunt and capture food for their babies.

Wasps have a swordlike stinger on the very end of their body, so they basically have a knife sticking out of their bums. Not only are their stingers sharp, but they are also reusable and coated with a venom that is extremely painful. A single angry wasp can sting you multiple times!

If that isn't bad enough, many wasps release a chemical smell, called a pheromone, when they get scared. This "odor" tells other nearby wasps that a nest member is in trouble and needs help. That's right, scare a wasp and it might call for back up! But before you run screaming every time you see a wasp, remember that wasps generally won't attack unless they feel threatened. So, if you leave them alone, they will leave you alone.

If you have a wasp nest on or near your home the safest thing to do is to hire a professional pest control person to remove the nest. But remember, these insects play an important role in maintaining balance in the ecosystem so the best policy is to let them be.

The cockroach is estimated to be at least 200 million years old. There are roach fossils dating back as far as 350 million years, so they actually predate some dinosaurs.

COCKROACHES

Have you ever flicked on a light in the middle of the night and seen something scatter fast? Maybe you were on your way to the kitchen for a midnight snack or perhaps you were heading to the bathroom . . . If there is one insect that most often surprises a scream out of us it is cockroaches.

What are cockroaches?

Cockroaches are winged, flat insects that inhabit every environment on the planet, from the poles to the tropics. Out of the 4,600 different types of cockroaches in the world, only 30 have moved into our homes and are considered pests. A pest in the scientific sense, is a destructive insect that attacks us, our food, or home.

WORLD'S WORST HOUSEMATES

As long as humans have had homes, there have been cockroaches living in them. Cockroaches can flatten their bodies to the thickness of two stacked coins, so they can fit through almost any crack or opening. You can't blame a cockroach for wanting to move into your home—it's warm, with plenty of places for a cockroach to live (like the space between walls and underneath the floors), not to mention all the food you provide!

Enthusiastic eaters

Cockroaches are enthusiastic eaters of everything. They are the opposite of a picky eater. They will eat human food, pet food, living and dead plants, books, wallpaper, and even fingernails and toenails. Lucky for us, the one thing they don't eat is human blood because they don't have the right mouthparts for it. Cockroach mouthparts are designed for chewing not sucking. Despite their love of food, cockroaches can survive for months without food or water.

Better tidy up

The dirtier the home and the more food that is left out, the more likely it is that cockroaches will move in. So, listen when an adult tells you to sweep up the crumbs or not leave dirty dishes in your room. These actions might just prevent cockroaches from moving in! If you do get some unwelcome friends moving in, the only other options are sticky traps, or special chemicals that kill cockroaches.

Cockroaches are social; they like to live in groups. They secrete pheromones, special smelly chemicals, so that other cockroaches can find the group or nearby food.

Did you know many cockroaches can make sounds? Some make buzzing noises using their wings while others can chirp using their mouths. There are even cockroaches that can make a hissing sound using their breathing holes.

Unwanted present

Cockroaches give their eggs a little bit of extra protection, wrapping them up like a lovely box of chocolates in a package called an *ootheca*. This egg case is sometimes glued to things like the underside of tables or beds, or it is dropped into cracks and crevices in dark and secluded places.

Find the difference

A baby cockroach hatches out of the egg case about one month after it is laid. Cockroaches undergo incomplete metamorphosis so baby cockroaches are called nymphs and they will molt a few more times before becoming an adult. You can always tell if you are dealing with a baby cockroach because it will not have wings.

Cockroaches reproduce at an incredible rate. If you start out with two cockroaches and gave them unlimited food, then in a year you would have a million cockroaches.

AS TOUGH AS CAN BE

Cockroaches are some of the toughest, most adaptable bugs around, which is why scientists have been studying them for years.

Indestructible insects

Scientist have attached tiny cameras to cockroaches to gather information from places humans can't (or don't want to) go. Cockroaches are able to survive incredibly high levels of radiation, live long periods of time without food or water, and withstand super high (100°F) and low (45°F) temperatures.

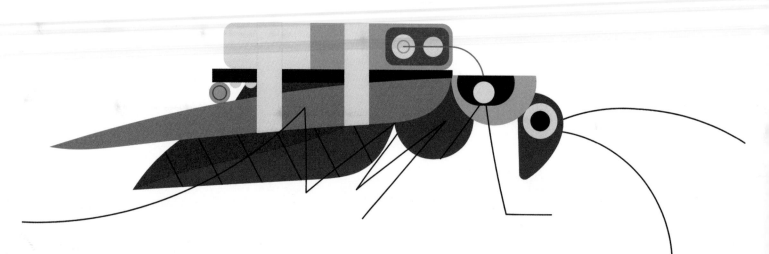

Chinese and American scientists have designed a robot [NP1] inspired by cockroaches. These scientists believe since cockroaches are small, difficult to squish, and can fit into narrow spaces they will make the perfect robot to help find people during natural disasters like earthquakes when buildings often collapse.

A cockroach named Nadezhda was sent into space by Russian scientists. The cockroach spent 12 days in space on the Foton-M bio-satellite before returning to Earth.

Fleas can be found wherever furry and feathered animals live. They can be spotted among the feathers of an emperor penguin in Antarctica, nestled in the fur of mice or hamsters in the desert, and can even be found flying by moonlight on the backs of bats.

FLEAS

There is nothing better than a warm, soft dog to cuddle with as you drift off to sleep. But when you wake up in the morning your legs are covered with itchy little red bumps. You search and search but can't find anything in your bed. What bit you and why? Well, it seems when your pooch joined you in bed last night he brought along a few tiny hungry friends called fleas.

What are fleas?

Chances are if you have a cat or a dog for a pet you treat them regularly for fleas so you may have never even seen one. Although to be fair, they are so tiny that even in a home infested with fleas you probably still might not see one. Adult fleas are about the size of a poppy seed and there are more than 2,500 different kinds of fleas.

SECOND CHOICE ON THE MENU

Fleas are not actually big fans of humans. They would rather feed on something with fur if they can. To fleas we are like broccoli, they will feed on us but only if nothing better is around.

Short and stout

What are fleas doing when they burrow into the fur, feather, nests, burrows, and hair of animals? They are using their short, stout proboscis (mouthpart) to suck blood. Just like mosquitoes and lice, fleas start feeding by spitting into you saliva that is full of "magical" chemicals that numb your skin. Only after spitting into you will a flea start sucking your blood.

Fleas have specially designed claws that are perfect for holding on to fur and feathers.

Blood buffet

Both female and male adult fleas feed on blood. Given a choice at the blood buffet, a flea will always choose a cat or a dog over a human. Similar to how you might choose ice cream and chocolate over broccoli. They have a specially designed piercing mouthpart, similar to a mosquito's but a little shorter, which is a perfect straw for sipping blood.

Guess who?

You can tell different kinds of fleas apart by the kind of mustaches they have. What? You didn't know fleas had mustaches? Well, the technical term for them is bristles, but you can imagine them as distinguished souls with mustaches (except both male and female fleas have these bristles.)

High jumpers

Fleas do not have wings, but these tiny insects can jump as high as 8 inches. That would be the equivalent of a person jumping over the Eiffel Tower while going as fast as a rocket ship.

Finding furry friends

Fleas find their hosts by sensing body heat, the vibrations caused by movement, and CO_2 from breathing. When the ground starts shaking from some huge (to a flea) animal moving around like a giant Godzilla, they start jumping towards the commotion. As the flea gets closer it senses and locates the perfect landing spot on its new furry friend and then begins feeding.

THE GREATEST SHOW ON EARTH!

In the 1830s, flea circuses were a popular form of entertainment. These shows featured fleas towing tiny miniature carts and chariots and were put on by watchmakers or jewelers to show off their skill at making miniature devices. Spectators would be ushered into tents to watch some of the smallest circus performers on the planet . . . fleas!

Up until around the 1940s it was quite common to share your home with fleas. But as hygiene improved and the vacuum cleaner was invented, human fleas became scarce and flea circuses gradually began to decline.

Flea

Flea

Today we've come to realize that it is
cruel for wild animals (and even fleas!)
to be trained to perform in circuses.

BREAK THE CYCLE

We humans love our pets but we do not love the small itchy dots of flea bites.
To be able to cuddle your kitten to your heart's content again without fear of getting
any itchy bites you have to interrupt the flea's life cycle at just the right moment . . .

Eggs-travaganza!

A female flea can lay up to 1,000 eggs in her
lifetime. She lays these eggs one at time and
uses her very strong hind legs to fling them far
away from her. These eggs are not sticky so they
will end up everywhere . . . and because they are
incredibly tiny, about the size of one of the ridges
on your finger, they are rarely noticed.

Unsavory appetites . . .

It takes a flea egg two to five days to hatch a
larva (the baby flea). These larvae are very small
wormlike creatures called maggots. They live
in whatever dark cracks and crevices they can
find and will pretty much eat anything, but their
favorite food in the world is the poop of adult
fleas. Yes, that is right . . . they eat poop.

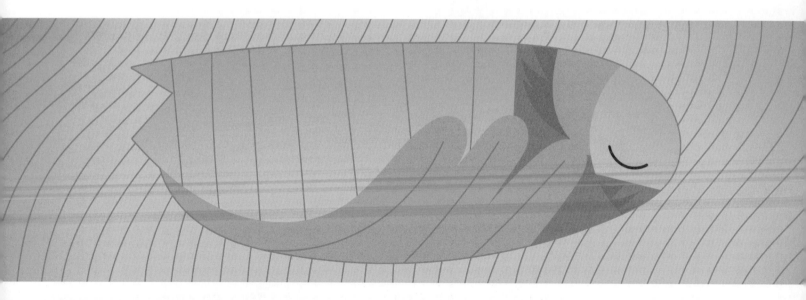

Clever camouflage

A flea larva will molt three times before forming a pupae. Flea pupae make their cocoons out of whatever
stuff is around them as a form of camouflage. So, if they are living in a home with a gray carpet, they will
make a cocoon made up of fibers from that gray carpet. They will spend two weeks in their cocoons before
emerging in their adult form. After that, all they need to do is find a furry friend to feed on and they are set.

How do we get rid of fleas?

We humans love our pets but we do not love flea bites. Each year the world spends billions of dollars getting rid of fleas because we really don't like to be itchy. What most people use is a chemical flea treatment that is applied to the fur of pets. This stops the fleas from molting, so they can't grow and reach adulthood.

If a flea larva hatches somewhere without enough food around, it has the amazing ability to go into sleep-mode. This insect version of hibernation is called diapause and allows flea larvae to survive for up to 200 days without food.

There are a lot of other kinds of insects (or bugs) that look like bedbugs. If you want to make sure it's NOT a bedbug, check for wings. If it has wings, it is not a bedbug!

Real bedbug

BEDBUGS

Good night, sleep tight, don't let the bedbugs bite! You might have heard this saying before you went to sleep but have you ever wondered what a bedbug actually is?

What are bedbugs?

Bedbugs are insects that feed only on the blood of mammals and birds, with two specific types of bedbugs that have evolved to feed primarily on humans. Bedbugs are smaller than the tip of a cotton swab and are incredibly flat. The body of a bedbug is as thin as a piece of paper, which is perfect for slipping in and out of nooks and crannies in our homes.

GREEDY EATERS

Bedbugs have big appetites and they like to take their time sucking up your blood. Adult male or female bedbugs will use their long proboscis to drink your blood for up to ten minutes at a time.

Adult bedbugs eat such big meals that they only feed every three to seven days. After they are done feeding, they return to their hiding spots to digest.

Blood, blood and more blood

About a week after a bedbug egg has been laid, a bedbug nymph will emerge out of the egg. Nymphs are the mini-adult forms of insects that undergo incomplete metamorphosis. Bedbug nymphs will molt five times, shedding their exoskeletons and getting slightly bigger each time, before becoming an adult. This process can take up to two months. Every stage of the life cycle of bedbugs feeds on blood, they just can't get enough of the stuff!

When a bedbug feeds it will eat up to three times its body weight in blood. Think about how much food you would need to eat to take in three times your body weight!

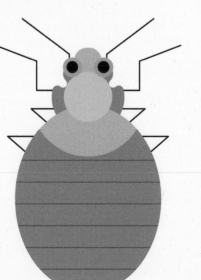

THERE'S NO HIDING!

Bedbugs will come out any time of the day or night if they sense a human is around. A lot of people think bedbugs are only active at night, like vampires, but that is not true. So, even if you leave all the lights on when you go to sleep, bedbugs will still find you.

Like mosquitoes, lice, and fleas, bedbugs find us by sensing CO_2 and heat. If they can sniff out your breath (CO_2) or sense your body heat they will leave their hiding spots and come out to feed. But how do they end up in your home in the first place?

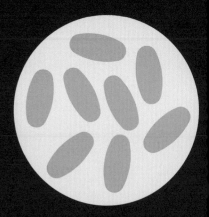

Female bedbugs will lay two to four eggs a day in whatever spot they are hiding. A female bedbug can live up to a year so that is a whole lot of eggs!

Despite their name, bedbugs don't only live in our beds. They can live in any space in our home that their very flat bodies can fit into.

Bedbugs don't have any wings and can't jump, which means their only way of moving around is crawling and boy do they crawl! Adult bedbugs can travel up to 100 feet a night to find a meal.

Bedbugs can live for up to a year without blood because they can undergo diapause (insect hibernation), so they are really hard to get rid of.

Since bedbugs don't live on our bodies it is usually our stuff that moves them around, things like backpacks, purses, and luggage. These are things that we set down in lots of places that would allow a little bedbug hitchhiker to climb aboard.

ANCIENT REMEDIES

Bedbugs have been around for a long time. Scientists think bedbugs evolved from bugs that used to feed on bats back when humans and bats lived together in caves. The oldest fossil evidence of human bedbugs is from 3,500 years ago.

Egyptologists have discovered records of bedbug treatments from Ancient Egypt almost 3,500 years ago. Bedbugs have even been found on the bodies of Egyptian mummies in their tombs.

The remains of bedbugs have been found in Roman archaeolgical sites from almost 2,500 years ago. The Romans believed eating crushed up bedbugs could cure poisonous snake bites.

Hundreds of years ago, people would stuff their beds with bean leaves or sprinkle bean leaves around their bed to prevent bedbugs. Bean leaves have tiny little hairs shaped like hooks that trap the legs of bedbugs and stop them from being able to crawl!

Did you know you can use dogs that have been specially trained to sniff out bedbugs? Today, to get rid of bedbugs we use specialized chemicals or machinery that makes houses really, really hot (above 115°F) as bedbugs can't survive hot temperatures.

ARE BUGS REALLY SO BAD?

After reading this book you might think that all insects are blood-sucking, itch-inducing, irritating nasty creatures but the truth is that the insects discussed here are just a tiny fraction of what exists in the world.

Right now, there are approximately 10 quintillion (10,000,000,000,000,000,000) individual beautiful insects living on planet Earth. Some insects help cycle nutrients into the soil by eating dead plant material. Other insects pollinate plants, helping to make fruit, and move seeds around. Insects also serve as a food source for lots of other creatures like fish, bats, birds, reptiles, and rodents. Without insects, our entire ecosystem would collapse, and while a few (like the ones in this book) are annoying, the majority have important and unique roles to play in nature that have nothing to do with humans.

GLOSSARY

A

Algae – A simple, nonflowering, plant that is usually found in water

Allergic – A negative reaction a human body can have to certain substances, e.g., plants or animals

Antenna – A long thin feeler on the head of certain insects' heads

Archaeologist – A scientist who studies human history and culture by digging up artifacts

B

Bacteria – Small living things that can be found in all natural environments

Blood clotting – An important process that prevents excessive bleeding when a blood vessel is injured

C

Cocoon – A covering made of soft threads that protects an insect during its pupal stage

Complete metamorphosis – A change in body form with four stages (egg, larva, pupa, and adult)

D

Diapause – Spontaneous interruption in the development of insects

Digest – To soften and change food in the stomach and intestines so the body can absorb it

E

Ecosystem – A community of interacting organisms and their environment

Entomologist – A person who studies insects

Exoskeleton – A hard covering that protects the body of some types of animals and insects

H

Haustellum – The sucking organ, or probiscis, of an insect

I

Incomplete metamorphosis – A change in body form with three stages (egg, nymph, and adult)

Infestation – An invasion of insects in a particular place

L

Larva – An insect in the first stage of its life after it hatches from an egg

M

Molting – To shed outer material, such as a shell

N

Nymph – The sexually immature form of an insect

P

Pheromone – Chemicals produced by animals that affect the behavior of other animals

Pollen – A substance produced by seed-bearing plants

Proboscis – The sucking organ of an insect, also used for piercing

Protein – One of the substances found in food that is essential to building muscle

Pupa – An insect in the stage of development where it is contained in and protected by a hard covering and does not move

R

Reproduce – The process by which living things produce offspring

S

Saliva – The watery fluid in the mouth made by the salivary glands

Siphon – A tubelike part of an insect that spends time underwater, which serves as a breathing tube

V

Venom – Poison produced by an animal

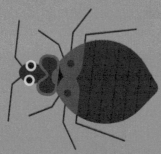

INDEX

To Lisa and Tanja who always remind me to
dream bigger, laugh louder, and be weirder
because life is too short for anything else.
– Nazzy Pakpour

For my nieces and nephews: Max, Henry,
Oliver, William, Isabel, Alyssia, and Albie.
– Owen Davey

First edition published in 2023 by Flying Eye Books Ltd.
27 Westgate Street, London, E8 3RL.

Text © Nazzy Pakpour 2023
Illustrations © Owen Davey 2023

Edited by Sara Forster
Designed by Sarah Crookes

1 3 5 7 9 10 8 6 4 2

Published in the US by Flying Eye Books Ltd.
Printed in China on FSC® certified paper.

ISBN: 978-1-83874-862-3

www.flyingeyebooks.com